NEVADA DMV TEST

PASS ON THE FIRST TIME

2019

1.   WHAT AGE MUST WEAR SEAT BELTS?

    a.   10 YEARS AND OLDER
    b.   15 YEARS AND OLDER
    c.   6 YEARS AND OLDER

2.   WHO MUST BE IN AN APPROVED CHILD RESTRAINT SYSTEM?
    a.   AGE 10 AND YOUNGER WEIGHING LESS THAN 100 POUNDS
    b.   AGE 6 AND YOUNGER WEIGHING LESS THAN 60 POUNDS
    c.   ANY CHILD UNDER 16

3.   SOMEONE MAY HOLD A CHILD ON THEIR LAP AT ANYTIME?
    a.   TRUE
    b.   FALSE

4.   YOU CAN NEVER BUCKLE TWO CHILDREN IN ONE SINGLE SAFTEY BELT?
    a.   TRUE
    b.   FALSE

5.   YOU ARE ALLOWED TO LEAVE A CHILD UNDER 7 UNATTENDED IN A VEHICLE IF THE CHILD IS WATCHED BY A PERSON AT LEAST 12 YEARS OF AGE?
    a.   TRUE
    b.   FALSE

6. YOU ARE ALLOWED TO LEAVE PETS IN YOUR VEHICLE DURING EXTREME COLD OR HEAT?
    a. TRUE
    b. FALSE

7. HOW SHOULD INFANTS BE PLACED IN A CAR SEAT?
    a. CAR SEAT FORWARD FACING
    b. CAR SEAT REAR FACING
    c. ON A SEAT OR LAP OF SOMEONE ELSE

8. CAN YOU PUT AN INFANT IN THE FRONT SEAT OF A CAR THAT HAS A PASSENGER SIDE AIRBAG?
    a. TRUE
    b. FALSE

9. BEFORE YOU START YOUR ENGINE YOU SHOULD
    a. ADJUST YOUR DRIVERS SEAT
    b. MAKE SURE WINDOWS ARE CLEAN
    c. BUCKLE UP
    d. CHECK YOUR ATTITUDE
    e. TURN ON HEADLIGHTS, WIPERS, AND SIGNALS IF NEEDED
    f. ALL OF THE ABOVE

10. WHAT ARE THE STEPS BEFORE YOU
MOVE YOUR VEHICLE?
    a. STOP AND LOOK FOR TRAFFIC
    b. STOP, LOOK, AND LISTEN FOR
       TRAFFIC, PEDESTRIANS, AND
       BICYCLISTS
    c. NOTHING JUST MOVE FORWARD

11. WHAT DOES A RED SIGN MEAN?
    a. GO
    b. SLOW DOWN
    c. STOP
    d. NO, DO NOT OR STOP

12. WHAT DOES A GREEN SIGN MEAN?
    a. STOP
    b. SLOW DOWN
    c. GO
    d. DIRECTION OR GUIDANCE

13. WHAT DOES A WHITE SIGN MEAN?
    a. LAW OR RULE, REGULATORY
    b. STOP
    c. GO
    d. NOTHING

14. WHAT DOES AN ORANGE SIGN MEAN?
    a. REPAIR WARNING, ROAD
       CONSTRUCTION
    b. SLOW DOWN
    c. STOP
    d. WARNING

15. WHAT DOES A BLUE SIGN MEAN?
    a. DRIVER SERVICES, EXAMPLE
       FOOD OR LODGING
    b. NOTHING
    c. GO
    d. STOP

16. WHAT DOES A BROWN SIGN MEAN?
    a. INFORMATION
    b. NOTHING
    c. GO
    d. STOP
    e. RECREATION OR SCENIC AREA
       INFORMATION

17. WHAT DOES AN OCTAGON SHAPE
    MEAN?
    a. GO
    b. STOP
    c. WARNING

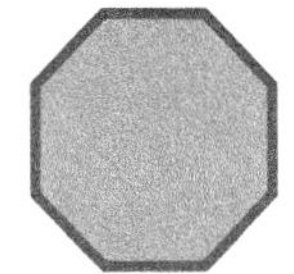

18. WHAT DOES A DIAMOND SHAPE MEAN?
    a. WARNING
    b. STOP
    c. GO
    d. NOTHING

19. WHAT DOES A RECTANGLE SHAPE
    MEAN?
    a. DIRECTIONS
    b. STOP
    c. GO
    d. NOTHING

20. WHAT DOES AN INVERTED TRIANGLE
MEAN?
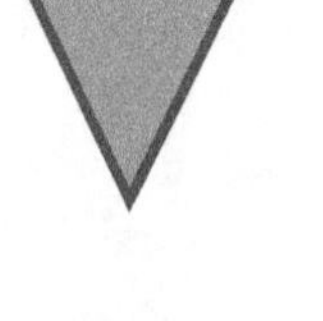
   a. STOP
   b. WARNING
   c. YIELD OR RIGHT OF WAY
   d. INFORMATION

21. WHAT DOES A PENNANT SHAPE MEAN?

   a. STOP
   b. WARNING
   c. NO PASSING
   d. INFORMATION

22. WHAT DOES A PENTAGON SHAPE MEAN?
   a. STOP
   b. RAILROAD
   c. SCHOOL ZONES AND SCHOOL
      CROSSING

23. WHAT DOES A CIRCLE SHAPE MEAN?
   a. SCHOOL ZONE
   b. RAILROAD CROSSING AHEAD
   c. STOP
   d. WARNING

24. WHAT DOES A CROSSBUCK SHAPE
MEAN?
   a. STOP
   b. SCHOOL ZONE
   c. ACTUAL RAILROAD CROSSING

25. WHAT DOES A SHIED SHAPE MEAN?
    a. ROUTE MARKER
    b. RAILROAD
    c. HOSPITAL

26. WHEN YOU COME TO A STOP SIGN YOU SHOULD
    a. COME TO A SLOW ROLLING STOP
    b. COME TO A COMPLETE STOP
    c. DON'T STOP AND JUST KEEP GOING
    d. COME TO A COMPLETE STOP AND LOOK BOTH WAYS

27. AT A 4 WAY STOP YOU MUST
    a. WAIT FOR ALL OTHER VEHICLES THAT ARE ALREADY AT THE INTERSECTION
    b. WAIT FOR THE VEHICLE TO THE LEFT OF YOU THEN GO
    c. DO NOTHING AND MOVE FORWARD

28. WHAT DOES A YIELD SIGN MEAN?
    a. SLOW DOWN AND MOVE FORWARD WHEN YOU ARE AT THE INTERSECTION
    b. DON'T GIVE PEDESTRIANS AND THROUGHT TRAFFIC THE RIGHT OF WAY
    c. SLOW DOWN AND GIVE OTHERS THE RIGHT OF WAY

29. YOU DO NOT HAVE TO OBEY
REGULATORY SIGNS?
    a. TRUE
    b. FALSE

30. IF THE TRAFFIC LIGHTS ARE NOT
WORKING YOU SHOULD
    a. GO THROUGH THE
        INTERSECTION
    b. COME TO A ROLLING STOP THEN
        PROCEED
    c. COME TO A FULL STOP THEN
        PROCEED
    d. JUST PROCEED WITH CAUTION

31. WHAT DOES A FLASHING RED LIGHT
MEAN?
    a. SLOW DOWN BUT PROCEED
    b. COME TO A FULL STOP AND ONLY
        GO WHEN CLEAR
    c. LOOK BUT KEEP DRIVING
        THROUGH THE INTERSECTION

32. YOU CAN MAKE A LEFT TURN AT A RED
LIGHT ONLY WHEN ARE YOU ARE
TURNING FROM A ONE- WAY STREET
ONTO ANOTHER ONE- WAY STREET
THAT HAS TRAFFIC MOVING TO THE
RIGHT?
    a. TRUE
    b. FALSE

33. PEDESTRIANS AT A RED LIGHT MUST

    a. CROSS AT ANYTIME
    b. CROSS IF NOONE IS COMING
    c. DO NOT CROSS UNLESS THE
        SIGNAL OR POLICE SAYS SO

34. PEDESTRIANS AT A YELLOW LIGHT MUST
    a. NOT START CROSSING THE
        STREET UNLESS A SIGNAL OR
        POLICE SAYS SO
    b. CROSS THE STREET FAST
    c. CROSS ONLY IF NOONE IS
        COMING

35. YOU DO NOT HAVE TO OBEY THE WALK
/ DON'T WALK SIGNS.
    a. TRUE
    b. FALSE

36. YOU CAN PASS ON A BROKEN OR
DASHED WHITE LINE MOVING IN THE
SAME DIRECTION?
    a. TRUE
    b. FALSE

37. YOU CAN NOT PASS ON A SOLID WHITE
LINE.
    a. TRUE
    b. FALSE

38. YELLOW LINES MEAN
   a. LANES OF TRAFFIC MOVING IN
      THE SAME DIRECTION
   b. LANES OF TRAFFIC MOVING IN
      THE OPPOSITE DIRECTION
   c. LANES OF TRAFFIC MOVING IN
      BOTH DIRECTIONS

39. YOU CAN NOT CROSS OVER OR PASS ON
    A SOLID YELLOW LINE?
   a. TRUE
   b. FALSE

40. DOUBLE YELLOW LINES MEAN
   a. YOU CAN NOT PASS IF THE LINES
      ON YOUR SIDE ARE SOLID
   b. YOU CAN NOT PASS IF THE LINES
      ON YOUR SIDE ARE SOLID
   c. YOU CAN PASS NO MATTER
      WHAT

41. CROSSWALK LINES MEAN YOU
   a. MUST KEEP DRIVING WITHOUT
      LOOKING
   b. MUST ALWAYS STOP YOUR
      VEHICLE BEFORE THE
      CROSSWALK
   c. MUST ALWAYS STOP YOUR
      VEHICLE IN THE CROSSWALK
   d. MUST ALWAYS STOP YOUR
      VEHICLE AFTER THE CROSSWALK

42. HOW MANY FEET FROM THE RAILROAD
TRACKS MUST YOU STOP YOUR
VEHICLE?
   a. 50 FEET
   b. 25 FEET
   c. 15 FEET

43. IN SCHOOL ZONES SPEED LIMITS ARE IN
EFFECT
   a. ALL DAY
   b. 3 HOURS BEFORE THE START OF
      SCHOOL
   c. 3 HOURS AFTER THE START OF
      SCHOOL
   d. 1/2 HOURS BEFORE SCHOOL
      STARTS TO ½ HOURS AFTER
      SCHOOL ENDS

44. YOU CAN MAKE A UTURN IN A SCHOOL
ZONE IF THERE IS NO SCHOOL, NO
CHILDREN ARE PRESENT, ½ HOUR
BEFORE SCHOOL AND ½ HOUR AFTER
SCHOOL, OR WHEN THE SCHOOL ZONE
LIGHTS ARE NOT IN EFFECT/
   a. TRUE
   b. FALSE

45. FAILURE TO YIELD THE RIGHT OF WAY IS
THE LEADING CAUSE OF ACCIDENTS IN
NEVADA.
   a. TRUE
   b. FALSE

46. NEVADA LAW DOESN'T REALLY GIVE
ANYONE THE RIGHT OF WAY.
    a. TRUE
    b. FALSE

47. WHEN YOU COME TO AN INTERSECTION
WHO GETS THE RIGHT OF WAY?
    a. VEHICLE ON YOUR RIGHT
    b. A VEHICLE ALREADY AT THE INTERSECTION
    c. VEHICLE GOING STRAIGHT AHEAD VERSE ONE THAT IS TURNING
    d. VEHICLES ENTERING A MAIN ROAD FROM A MINOR ROAD
    e. ALL OF THE ABOVE

48. WHEN AN EMERGENCY VEHICLE IS
PRESENT YOU MUST GIVE RIGHT OF
WAY TO THEM?
    a. TRUE
    b. FALSE

49. PEDESTRIANS IN CROSSWALKS AND
INTERSECTIONS HAVE THE RIGHT OF
WAY OVER VEHICLES?
    a. TRUE
    b. FALSE

50. DRIVING TOO SLOW UNSAFE.
    a. TRUE
    b. FALSE

51. FREEWAYS ARE THE SAFEST ROADS.
    a. TRUE
    b. FALSE

52. WHEN ENTERING A FREEWAY, YOU MUST
    a. LOOK FOR AN OPENING IN TRAFFIC AND USE YOUR TURN SIGNAL TO ENTER THE HIGHWAY
    b. YIELD TO TRAFFIC ALREADY ON THE FREEWAY
    c. LEAVE THE EXTREME LEFT LANE FOR FASTER TRAFFIC
    d. STAY ALERT
    e. ALL OF THE ABOVE

53. IF A FREEWAY ENTRANCE HAS RAMP METERS AND ARE SWITCHED ON YOU MUST
    a. PULL UP AND STOP ON RED
    b. BE ALERT
    c. WAIT FOR THE GREEN LIGHT
    d. DO NOTHING AND MOVE FORWARD
    e. A, B, AND C

54. WHEN EXITING A FREEWAY, YOU MUST
    a. CHECK IN FRONT AND BEHIND YOU
    b. SIGNAL AND MOVE INTO THE PROPER EXIT LANE
    c. BACK UP IF YOU MISS THE EXIT RAMP
    d. A AND B

55. WHAT DOES ABS STAND FOR?
    a. AUTOMATIC BRAKE SYSTEM
    b. ANTI LOCKING BRAKE SYSTEM
    c. ABCS

56. THERE ARE THREE TYPES OF ABE SYSTEMS?
    a. TRUE
    b. FALSE

57. YOUR STOPPING DISTANCE DEPENDS ON
    a. TYPE OF VEHICLE
    b. SPEED
    c. CONDITION OF VEHICLE
    d. WEATHER
    e. A, B, D
    f. ALL OF THE ABOVE

58. REACTION TIME INCREASES AS DRIVING DECISIONS BECOME EASIER.
    a. TRUE
    b. FALSE

59. NORMAL REACTION TIMES ARE
   a.   5 SECONDS
   b.   10 SECONDS
   c.   2.5 SECONDS
   d.   2 – 2.5 SECONDS

60. IF YOU DOUBLE YOUR SPEED YOUR
   BRAKING DISTANCE BECOMES 4 TIMES
   AS FAR?
   a.   TRUE
   b.   FALSE

61. WHEN YOU ARE DEFENSIVE DRIVING
   YOU
   a.   LOOK AHEAD AT ALEAST 12
        SECONDS
   b.   LOOK AHEAD AT LEAST 5
        SECONDS
   c.   DO NOTHING
   d.   DRIVE ANGRY

62. THE MINIMUM FOLLOWING DISTANCE
   BETWEEN CARS WHEN DRIVING 40
   MILES PER HOUR.
   a.   1 SECOND
   b.   10 SECONDS
   c.   2 SECONDS
   d.   5 SECONDS

63. THE USE OF CELL PHONES OR
HANDHELD WIRELESS DEVICES ARE
ALLOWED WHILE DRIVING IN
EMERGENCIES.
    a. TRUE
    b. FALSE

64. IF YOU SEE RED FLASHING LIGHTS IN
YOUR REVIEW MIRROR YOU NEED TO
    a. GO FASTER
    b. PULL OVER AND STOP IN THE
        MIDDLE OF THE ROAD
    c. PULL OVER TO THE SIDE OUR OF
        TRAFFIC AND STOP
    d. DO NOTHING

65. WHAT IS A ROUNDABOUT?
    a. A CIRCLE
    b. A TYPE OF CAR
    c. A LARGER CIRCULAR AREA IN THE
        MIDDLE OF AN INTERSECTION
        MEANT TO CONTROL THE RIGHT
        OF WAY OF VEHICLES

66. WHEN YOU APPROACH A ROUNDABOUT
YOU SHOULD USE THE RIGHT LANE TO
TURN LEFT, COMPLETE A UTURN OR GO
STRAIGHT?
    a. TRUE
    b. FALSE

67. WHAT DOES IT MEAN IF SOMEONE PUTS
THEIR LEFT ARM OUT OF THE WINDOW
POINTING STRAIGHT?

    a. RIGHT TURN
    b. LEFT TURN
    c. NOTHING
    d. BOTH
    e. STOP

68. WHAT DOES IT MEAN IF SOMEONE PUTS
THEIR LEFT ARM OUT OF THE WINDOW
BENT WITH HAND POINTING UPWARD?

    a. LEFT TURN
    b. RIGHT TURN
    c. NOTHING
    d. BOTH
    e. STOP

69. WHAT DOES IT MEAN IF SOMEONE PUTS
    THEIR LEFT ARM OUT OF THE
    WINDOWN BENT WITH HAND POINTING
    DOWNWARD?

    a. LEFT TURN
    b. RIGHT TURN
    c. NOTHING
    d. BOTH
    e. STOP

70. WHEN TURNING RIGHT YOU MUST BE IN
    THE FAR-LEFT TRAVEL LANE.
    a. TRUE
    b. FALSE

71. WHEN YOU WANT TO CHANGE LANES
    a. USE YOUR SIDE MIRRORAS ONLY
        TO CHECK TRAFFIC
    b. USE YOUR SIDE AND REAR
        MIRRORS TO CHECK TRAFFIC
    c. CHECK BLIND SPOTS
    d. DO NOT CHANGE LANES IN AN
        INTERSECTION
    e. B, C, AND D

72. UTURNS ARE ALLOWED ON ANY ROAD WHEN THEY ARE DONE SAFELY.
    a. TRUE
    b. FALSE

73. YOU CAN NOT MAKE A UTURN IF
    a. ON CURVES
    b. ON STRAIGHT ROAD
    c. ON A DIRT ROAD

74. PASSING IS SAFE ON TWO LANE ROADS IF
    a. YOU CAN CLEARLY SEE
    b. YOU CAN GO FASTER THEN THE OTHER VEHICLE
    c. THERE IS A SOLID YELLOW LINE

75. YOU CAN NOT PASS ON A TWO- LANE ROAD WHEN
    a. YOU ARE COMING TO A CURVE
    b. YOU ARE WITHIN A 100 FEET OF A STREET CROSSING
    c. THERE IS A SIGN PROHIBITING
    d. THERE IS A DOUBLE YELLOW LINE
    e. ALL OF THE ABOVE

76. YOU MAY PASS ON THE RIGHT IF THE
STREET OR HIGHWAY IS CLEARLY
MARKED FOR TWO OR MORE LANES OF
TRAFFIC MOVING IN THE SAME
DIRECTION BUT ONLY WHEN PASSING IS
SAFE.
   a. TRUE
   b. FALSE

77. WHEN YOU PASS A CYCLIST OR
MOTORIST YOU MUST BE AT LEAST
   a. 10 FEET AWAY FROM MOTORIST
   b. 5 FEET AWAY FROM MOTORIST
   c. 3 FEET AWAY FROM MOTORIST

78. IF YOU ARE PASSING PARKED CARS YOU
MUST LOOK OUT FOR
   a. VEHICLES WITH TURN SIGNALS
      ON
   b. VEHICLES WITH BACK UPLIGHTS
      ON
   c. VEHICLES WITH BRAKE LIGHTS
      ON
   d. EXHAUST COMING OU
   e. ALL OF THE ABOVE

79. WHEN PARKING YOUR VEHICLE YOUR
VEHICLE SHOULD FACE THE OPPOSITE
DIRECTION THAT NORMAL TRAFFIC
FLOWS.
   a. TRUE
   b. FALSE

80. YOU SHOULD NEVER TURN YOUR
    VEHICLE IGNITION TO THE LOCK
    POSITION WHILE STILL IN MOTION.
    a. TRUE
    b. FALSE

81. WHEN YOU PARK YOUR VEHICLE YOU
    a. TURN OFF THE ENGINE
    b. PUT ON THE EMERGENCY BRAKE
    c. GET OUT AND LEAVE THE CAR
        UNLOCKED
    d. NOTHING
    e. A AND B

82. WHEN YOU PARK ON A HILL WITHOUT
    A CURB YOU NEED TO TURN YOUR
    FRONT TIRES TO THE RIGHT.
    a. TRUE
    b. FALSE

83. WHEN YOU PARK ON A HILL WITH A
    CURB YOU NEED TO TURN YOUR FRONT
    TIRES TO THE LEFT
    a. TRUE
    b. FALSE

84. WHEN YOU PARK DOWNHILL YOU TURN
    YOUR TIRES TO FACE TRAFFIC.
    a. TRUE
    b. FALSE

85. YOU ARE ALLOWED TO PARK YOUR CAR
ON A SIDEWALK
    a.   TRUE
    b.   FALSE

86. YOU CAN PARK YOUR CAR 10 FEET FROM
A FIRE HYDRANT.
    a.   TRUE
    b.   FALSE

87. YOU CAN NOT PARK YOUR CAR
    a.   IN A TUNNEL OR ON A BRIDGE
    b.   IN A HANDICAP PARKING SPACE
    c.   IN A BICYCLE LANE
    d.   NEXT TO A CONSTRUCTION ZONE
    e.   ALL OF THE ABOVE

88. IN AN EMERGENCY YOU MUST
    a.   PULL OVER ON THE SIDE OF THE
         ROAD AND PUT YOUR 4 WAY
         FLASHERS ON
    b.   STOP IN THE ROAD AND PUT ON
         YOU FLASHERS
    c.   WALK ON THE FREEWAY

89. HEADLIGHTS ARE REQUIRED
    a. FROM 1 HOUR AFTER SUNSET
        UNTIL 1 HOUR BEFORE SUNRISE
    b. FROM ½ HOUR AFTER SUNSET
        UNTIL ½ HOUR BEFORE SUNRISE
    c. NEVER
    d. WHENEVER VEHICLES CANNOT
        BE CLEARLY SEEN WITHIN 1,000
        FEET
    e. B AND D

90. YOU NEED TO USE YOUR HEADLIGHTS
    WHEN YOU DRIVE IN THE RAIN, SNOW,
    OR FOG.
    a. TRUE
    b. FALSE

91. WHEN YOU ARE DRIVING IN BAD
    WEATHER YOU MUST DRIVE FASTER.
    a. TRUE
    b. FALSE

92. STUDDED SNOW TIRES MAY ONLY BE
    USED FROM OCTOBER 1ST THROUGH
    APRIL 30TH.
    a. TRUE
    b. FALSE

93. TIRES WITH TRACTABLE STUDS ARE
ALLOWED ANY TIME OF THE YEAR BUT
THE STUDS CAN ONLY BE ENGAGED
DURING OCTOBER 1ST THROUGH APRIL
30TH.
   a. TRUE
   b. FALSE

94. SKIDDING HAPPENS DURING SUNNY DRY
DAYS.
   a. TRUE
   b. FALSE

95. IF YOUR BRAKES FAIL YOU NEED TO
   a. PANIC
   b. CALL 911
   c. PUMP THE BRAKE PEDAL
   d. CALL YOUR PARENTS

96. IF YOU DRIVE THROUGH WATER YOU
SHOULD DRY YOUR BRAKES BY
APPLYING LIGHT PRESSURE TO BRAKE
PEDALS TO DRY THEM.
   a. TRUE
   b. FALSE

97. IF YOUR WINDSHIELD WIPERS FAIL YOU
SHOULD KEEP DRIVING.
   a. TRUE
   b. FALSE

98. IF YOUR GAS PEDAL STICKS
    a. QUICKLY PRESS YOUR FOOT
       HARD AGAINST THE PEDAL AND
       KEEP IT THERE
    b. QUICKLY PRESS YOUR FOOT
       HARD AGAINST THE PEDAL AND
       QUICKLY RELEASE IT
    c. SHIFT TO NEUTRAL
    d. APPLY BRAKES
    e. PLACE YOUR VEHICLE IN PARK
    f. B AND C
    g. B, C, AND D

99. IF YOUR HEADLIGHTS FAIL TURN ON
    YOUR PARKING LIGHTS OR 4 WAY
    FLASHERS TO GUIDE YOU SAFELY TO
    THE SIDE OF THE ROAD
    a. TRUE
    b. FALSE

100.   IF YOU SEE SMOKE FROM UNDER
    YOUR HOOD
    a. KEEP DRIVING UNTIL YOU GET
       HOME
    b. USE WATER TO PUT IT OUT
    c. SLOW DOWN, PULL OFF THE
       ROAD, AND SHUT OFF THE
       VEHICLE

101. IF YOUR STEERING FAILS

    a. SLOW DOWN AND APPLY THE BRAKES

    b. USE YOUR 4 WAY FLASHERS

    c. FREAK OUT

    d. NOTHING

    e. A AND B

102. IF YOU VEHICLE DRIFTS TO ANOTHER LANE STAY CALM, SLOW DOWN, STAY ON SHOULDER UNTIL YOU GET YOUR VEHICLE UNDER CONTROL.

    a. TRUE

    b. FALSE

103. WHAT IS A BLOWOUT?

    a. WHEN YOU ARE REALLY ANGRY

    b. WHEN THE TIRE SUDDENLLY LOSES AIR

    c. WHEN THE CAR CATCHES ON FIRE

104. IF YOU HAVE A BLOW OUT YOU MUST ACCELERATE AND MOVE YOUR CAR INTO THE OTHER LANE WITH CARS IN IT.

    a. TRUE

    b. FALSE

105. IF YOU HAVE A FLOODED ENGINE YOU SHOULD PRESS THE GAS PEDAL TO THE FLOOR AND RUN THE STARTER FOR SHORT INTERVALS OF 10-15 SECONDS.
    a. TRUE
    b. FALSE

106. LESS THAN ONE INCH OF RAIN CAUSES DRIVERS TO LOSE CONTROL OF THE VEHICLE
    a. TRUE
    b. FALSE

107. MOST VEHICLES FLOAT IN 2 FEET OF WATER OR LESS.
    a. TRUE
    b. FALSE

108. CARS TRAVELING AT A HIGH RATE OF SPEED CAN BE PUSHED OFF THE ROAD BY 6 INCHES OF WATER.
    a. TRUE
    b. FALSE

109. IF YOU ENCOUNTER A FLOODED AREA
    a. YOU SHOULD TRY TO DRIVE THORUGH IT
    b. GET OUT OF THE CAR AND SWIM
    c. FIND ANOTHER ROUTE TO TRAVEL

110. WORK ZONES ARE IDENTIFIED BY
ORANGE SIGNS, CONES, AND BARRELS.
   a. TRUE
   b. FALSE

111. WHEN YOU REACH A WORK ZONE YOU
MUST
   a. SLOW DOWN
   b. SPEED UP
   c. COME TO A STOP

112. WHEN APPROACHING A STOPPED
EMERGENCY VEHICLE
   a. GO FASTER
   b. SLOW DOWN
   c. BE PREPARED TO STOP
   d. MOVE TO A DIFFERENT LANE
       AWAY FROM THE VEHICLE
   e. B, C, AND D

113. WHAT IS A NO ZONE?
   a. SOMEWHERE YOU CAN'T DRIVE
   b. IN FRONT OF A COMMERCIAL
       TRUCK
   c. THE AREA IN BACK OF A
       COMMERCIAL VEHICLE WHERE
       THE VEHICLE CAN NOT SEE YOU

114. YOU SHOULD ALWAYS HANG OUT ON
THE SIDES OF COMMERCIAL VEHICLES.
   a. TRUE
   b. FALSE

115. WHEN PASSING A COMMERCIAL
    VEHICLE, YOU SHOULD CUT IN FRONT
    OF THEM.
        a. TRUE
        b. FALSE

116. YOU SHOULD NEVER PASS A
    COMMERCIAL VEHICLE THAT IS
    BACKING UP.
        a. TRUE
        b. FALSE

117. COMMERCIAL TRUCKS MAKE WIDE
    RIGHT TURNS,
        a. TRUE
        b. FALSE

118. MOTORCYCLIST CAN USE A COMPLETE
    LANE.
        a. TRUE
        b. FALSE

119. YOU CAN ALWAYS TELL HOW FAST A
    MOTORCYCLE IS GOING.
        a. TRUE
        b. FALSE

120. WHEN APPROACHING A MOTOCYCLE
FROM BEHIND
    a. BEEP AT THEM
    b. FLASH YOUR LIGHTS
    c. DIM YOUR HEADLIGHTS
    d. DO NOTHING

121. YOU NEED A SPECIAL MOTOCYCLE
ENDORSEMENT TO DRIVE A
MOTORCYCLE.
    a. TRUE
    b. FALSE

122. MOPED CAN RIDE IN ANY LANE.
    a. TRUE
    b. FALSE

123. MOPED OWNERS NEVER HAVE TO
REGISTER THEIR MOPEDS WITH THE
DMV.
    a. TRUE
    b. FALSE

124. YOU ARE NOT REQUIRED TO STOP FOR
SCHOOL BUSES WHO ARE LOADING AND
UNLOADING CHILDREN.
    a. TRUE
    b. FALSE

125. IF YOU ARE ON A DIVIDED ROAD WITH A
CONCRETE DIVIDER YOU DON'T HAVE
TO STOP FOR A SCHOOL BUS UNLESS IT
IS ON YOUR SIDE OF THE ROAD.
    a.   TRUE
    b.   FALSE

126. CYCLISTS CAN RIDE IN A TRAFFIC LANE
    a.   TRUE
    b.   FALSE

127. WHEN PASSING A BICYCLIST, YOU MUST
GO FAST AND CLOSE.
    a.   TRUE
    b.   FALSE

128. MOTORISTS AND CYCLISTS HAVE
EQUAL RIGHT TO USE ROADWAYS.
    a.   TRUE
    b.   FALSE

129. CYCLISTS MUST WEAR A HELMET.
    a.   TRUE
    b.   FALSE

130. CYCLISTS CAN WEAR A HEADSET.
    a.   TRUE
    b.   FALSE

131. IF YOU ARE UNDER 18 YOU CAN RIDE IN
THE BACK OF THE TRUCK IN THE BED.
    a.   TRUE
    b.   FALSE

132. PEDESTRIANS HAVE THE RIGHT OF WAY
    a. AT INTERSECTIONS
    b. WHERE CROSSWALKS EXISTS
    c. RAILROADS
    d.   A AND B
    e. NEVER

133. NON-COMMERCIAL DRIVERS CAN TOW UP TO 10,000 POUNDS OR LESS WITH A TOTAL LENGTH OF NO MORE THAN 70 FEET.
    a. TRUE
    b. FALSE

134. WHAT IS GVW?
    a. GROSS VEHICLE WEIGHT
    b. GRAND VEHICLE WEIGHT
    c. GROSS VITAL WEIGHT

135. TIRE LOAD IS
    a. THE WEIGHT OF THE TIRE
    b. THE SAFE WEIGHT A TIRE CAN CARRY AT SPECIFIED PRESSURE
    c. THE TREAD OF THE TIRE

136. WHEN TOWING YOU MUST GO AROUND
TURNS FAST AND KEEP THE CARGO AS
HIGH AS POSSIBLE.
    a. TRUE
    b. FALSE

137. A BALL AND HITCH COUPLER IS USED
FOR A MOTORCYCLE.
    a. TRUE
    b. FALSE

138. A FIFTH WHEEL HITCH IS MOUNTED TO
THE HOOD OF A CAR.
    a. TRUE
    b. FALSE

139. YOU MUST ALWAYS INSPECT YOUR
TRAILER PRE-TRIP AND WITHIN 50 MILES
AFTER BEGINNING THE TRIP.
    a. TRUE
    b. FALSE

140.   TOWING SAFELY MEANS
    a. BE AWARE OF YOUR
        SURROUNDINGS
    b. USE MIRRORS
    c. SIGNAL YOUR INTENTIONS
    d. COMMUNICATE YOUR PRESENCE
    e. ALL OF THE ABOVE

141. EMPTY TRUCKS REQUIRE GREATER
     STOPPING DISNTANCES BECAUSE THEY
     HAVE LESS TRACTION.
     a.   TRUE
     b.   FALSE

142. RIGHT TURNS WITH TRAILERS
     a.   ARE BEST DONE BY TURNING
          WIDE KEEPING REAR OF TRAILER
          TOWARDS CURB
     b.   ARE BEST DONE BY GOING SLOW
     c.   TURNING TO THE LEFT FIRST

143. WHEN TURNING LEFT WITH A TRAILER
     REACH THE MIDDLE OF THE
     INTERSECTION BEFORE STARTING YOUR
     TURN.
     a.   TRUE
     b.   FALSE

144. WHEN A TRAILER IS EMPTY IT IS MORE
     LIKELY TO SWING AROUND IF THE
     TRALER SKIDS AND LOCKS UP.
     a.   TRUE
     b.   FALSE

145. YOU CAN RECOGNIZE A TRAILER SKID BY
     LOOKING IN YOUR MIRRORS.
     a.   TRUE
     b.   FALSE

146.   IF A TRAILER SKIDS YOU SHOULD RELEASE THE BRAKES TO GET TRACTION BACK.
    a. TRUE
    b. FALSE

147. INSURANCE FOR YOUR VEHICLE IS REQUIRED IN NEVADA.
    a. TRUE
    b. FALSE

148. MINIMUM STATE COVERAGE FOR INSURANCE IS
    a. 25,000 BODILY INJURY OR DEATH OF A PERSON IN ONE ACCIDENT
    b. 50,000 BODILY INJURY OR DEATH OF TWO OR MORE PERSONS IN ONE ACCIDENT
    c. 20,00 FOR INJURY OR DESTRUCTION TO PROPERTY IN ONE ACCIDENT
    d. ALL OF THE ABOVE

149.   IF YOU ARE INVOLVED IN AN ACCIDENT OF $750 OR MORE DAMAGES YOU MUST COMPLETE A REPORT OF ACCIDENT FORM WITHIN 10 DAYS TO NV DMV.
    a. TRUE
    b. FALSE

150. IF YOU DO NOT REPORT AN ACCIDENT
TO DMV YOUR LICENSE CAN BE
SUSPENDED
   a. TRUE
   b. FALSE

151. AN SR22 IS A FORM OF LIABILITY
INSURANCE THAT THE DMV MONITORS
A PERSON WHO HAS HAD A SUSPENDED
LICENSE.
   a. TRUE
   b. FALSE

152. IF YOU HAVE A CRASH
   a. STOP
   b. WARN TRAFFIC AND GET
      MEDICAL HELP
   c. NOTIFY LAW ENFORCEMENT
   d. LEAVE THE SCENE
   e. A, B, AND C
   f. NOTHING

153. IF YOU RECEIVE 5 OR MORE POINTS IN A
12 MONTH PERIOD YOUR LICENSE WILL
BE SUSPENDED,
   a. TRUE
   b. FALSE

154. YOU CAN REMOVE 3 POINTS BY
ATTENDING TRAFFIC SCHOOL.
   a. TRUE
   b. FALSE

155. IT IS ILLEGAL TO GIVE FALSE INFMRATON WHEN APPLYING FOR A LICENSE AND LEND IT TO SOMEONE ELSE.
   a. TRUE
   b. FALSE

156. WHAT IS THE LEGAL ALCOHOL LIMIT?
   a. 1.0
   b. .09
   c. .08
   d. 1.1

157. IT IS LEGAL TO DRIVE UNDER THE INFLUENCE OF MARIJUANA.
   a. TRUE
   b. FALSE

158. IF YOU FAIL TO SUBMIT A BLOOD, BREATH, OR URINE TEST TO TEST FOR DRUGS OR ALCOHOL YOUR LICENSE WILL BE REVOKED AND YOU WILL NOT BE ELIGIBLE FOR A LICENSE FOR ONE YEAR FOR FIRST OFFENSE AND 3 YEARS FOR REVOKED IN THE PRIOR 7 YEARS.
   a. TRUE
   b. FALSE

159. IF YOU SHOW MORE THAN .08% LIMIT YOUR LICENSE WILL BE REVOKED.
   a. TRUE
   b. FALSE

160.   IF YOU HAVE MORE THAN .04%
BUT LESS THAN .08% ALCOHOL LIMIT
YOUR LICENSE WILL BE SUSPENDED FOR
90 DAYS.
   a. TRUE
   b. FALSE

161. A .02% ALCOHOL CONENTRATION
UNDER 21 YEARS OF AGE YOUR LICENSE
WILL BESUSPENDED FOR 90 DAYS.
   a. TRUE
   b. FALSE

162. IF YOU HAVE A COMMERICIAL DRIVER
LICNESE AND ANY AMOUNT OF AOCHOL
IS DETECTED YOURDRIVING PRIVELAGE
WILL BE AFFECTED.
   a. TRUE
   b. FALSE

163. FIRST TIME DUI OFENDERS WILLS EVE A
MINIMUMM OF ONE YEAR REVOCATION
FO NO LESS THAN 185 DAYS.
   a. TRUE
   b. FALSE

164.   YOUR LICENSE CAN BE
REINSTATED IF YOU HAD A DUI IF YOU
HAVE AN IGNITION INTERLOCK
RESTRICTION DEVICE AND IT IS
INSTALLED IN YOUR VEHICLE
   a. TRUE
   b. FALSE

165. YOU CAN DRIVE WITH AN OPEN
     CONTAINER OF ALCOHOL IN YOUR
     VEHICLE
     a. TRUE
     b. FALSE

166.   YOU CAN LOSE YOUR DRIVING
     PROVELAGES
     a. BY POINTS
     b. DRIVING UNDER THE INFLUENCE
     c. FAILURE TO APPEAR ON A TICKET
         IN COURT
     d. NOT MAINTING INSURANCE
     e. DRIVING SAFELY
     f. FOLLOWING RULES
     g. A, B, C, AND D

167. OUT OF STATE INSURANCE IS
     ACCEPTED.
     a. TRUE
     b. FALSE

168.   A PASSING SMOG CHECK IS
     REQUIRED FOR REGISTRATION IN
     NEVADA.
     a. TRUE
     b. FALSE

<u>ANSWER KEY</u>

1. C
2. B
3. B
4. A
5. A
6. B
7. B
8. B
9. F
10. B
11. D
12. D
13. A
14. A
15. A
16. E
17. B
18. A
19. A
20. C
21. C
22. C
23. B
24. C
25. A
26. D
27. A
28. C
29. B
30. C

31.   B
32.   B
33.   C
34.   A
35.   B
36.   A
37.   A
38.   B
39.   A
40.   A
41.   B
42.   C
43.   D
44.   A
45.   A
46.   A
47.   E
48.   A
49.   A
50.   A
51.   A
52.   E
53.   E
54.   D
55.   B
56.   B
57.   E
58.   B
59.   D
60.   A
61.   A
62.   C
63.   B

64.	C
65.	C
66.	B
67.	B
68.	B
69.	E
70.	B
71.	F
72.	A
73.	A
74.	A
75.	E
76.	A
77.	C
78.	E
79.	B
80.	A
81.	E
82.	A
83.	A
84.	B
85.	B
86.	B
87.	E
88.	A
89.	E
90.	A
91.	B
92.	A
93.	A
94.	B
95.	C
96.	A

97.	B
98.	G
99.	A
100.	C
101.	E
102.	A
103.	B
104.	B
105.	A
106.	A
107.	A
108.	A
109.	C
110.	A
111.	A
112.	E
113.	C
114.	B
115.	B
116.	A
117.	A
118.	A
119.	B
120.	C
121.	A
122.	B
123.	B
124.	B
125.	A
126.	A
127.	B
128.	A
129.	A

130.   B
131.   B
132.   D
133.   A
134.   A
135.   B
136.   B
137.   B
138.   B
139.   A
140.   E
141.   A
142.   A
143.   A
144.   A
145.   A
146.   A
147.   A
148.   D
149.   A
150.   A
151.   A
152.   E
153.   A
154.   A
155.   A
156.   C
157.   B
158.   A
159.   A
160.   A
161.   A
162.   A

163.   D
164.   A
165.   A
166.   B
167.   G
168.   B
169.   A

www.ingramcontent.com/pod-product-compliance
Lightning Source LLC
Chambersburg PA
CBHW051013050726
47592CB00007B/2826